STOLEN PLUMS

Stolen Plums

ALICE TURSKI

THE POETRY IMPRINT AT VÉHICULE PRESS

Published with the generous assistance of the Canada Council for the Arts and the Canada Book Fund of the Department of Canadian Heritage.

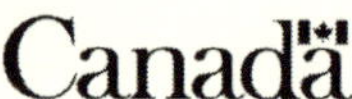

Signal Editions Editor: Michael Prior

Cover design by David Drummond
Photo of the author by LeithenMcGonigle
Set in Minion and Filosofia by Simon Garamond
Printed by Rapido Books

Dépôt légal, Library and Archives Canada and the Bibliothèque national du Québec, first trimester 2025

Library and Archives Canada Cataloguing in Publication

Title: Stolen plums / Alice Turski.
Names: Turski, Alice, author.
Identifiers: Canadiana (print) 20250114666 | Canadiana (ebook) 20250114690 | ISBN 9781550656770 (softcover) | ISBN 9781550656824 (EPUB)
Subjects: LCGFT: Poetry.
Classification: LCC PS8639.U775 S76 2025 | DDC C811/.6—dc23

Published by Véhicule Press, Montréal, Québec, Canada
vehiculepress.com

Distribution in Canada by LitDistCo
litdistco.ca

Distribution in the U.S. by Independent Publishers Group
ipgbook.com

Printed in Canada on FSC certified paper.

CONTENTS

I

Let It Simply Be So

A woman calls out of the blue to tell me
about her open sores. How they are turning black
and crawling with worms. *Fleeing*, she says, *fleeing*
for their lives. When they hit the floor
she always steps on them, but still they
jump. She is worried they know better,
that her body will be no good
soon—no good for masturbation,
no good for hibernation.
She calls because she thinks I am
the god of parasites. She woke up
one day and the worms had spelled
my name on her pillow. It's true, I have
always liked humbler things, things
that cling, things that can never be alone,
insecure things. But my flock is big,
I tell her that. I cannot possibly
remember which body is hers,
which worms, hers.

We Who Devour Pretty Things

When my lover points to three small flowers
at a corner of his family estate and says, *Look,*
the snowdrops have opened, I'm supposed
to know what this means. What *the snowdrops*
have opened is meant to do to my orbicularis oculi,
or my levator angular oris, and when no muscle
within me tenses or relaxes as it is meant to do,
his look gains intensity. The air of his estate
becomes thicker. The blades of grass of his estate
become agitated and a mourning dove comes crashing
down three feet to our right, cooing in panic
because its wings have stopped working.
Though spring is here, I feel not so different
from the time he left a hard gourd in my hands
at checkout, or the time he rubbed mink
on my boots. When fall is here, we'll pour boiling
water on the bricks and scatter baking soda
on the shingles, a chemistry for drowning
moss's short tendrils, but till then, when I get low
to the ground and examine my three-petaled harbinger,
I'll whisper in the hollow of her crooked throat,
I would have named you snowbell, and wonder
who taught him that this flower means more
when I learned wading through lilies at the botanical
garden, parting sodden creatures with the reeds
so that my mother could reach into the murky
depths of a duck pond and pull up, by the scruff
of its neck, an alien green pod that looked,
with its multiple eyes, so frightened.
When she tore its husk in two,

the carnage tasted like spring water.
Later, when we learned that the sparkle
on our arms were eggs belonging
to a whirligig beetle laid beneath
wide lily pads for cover, I wished
I could duck back into the rushes,
replace one dying bloom with another,
pin the meadowlark squawking above us
with a stone and set my mother sailing
to a land where food was not so plenty,
where water lilies grew without warrant
and my mother's teeth grew sharp
to save us all. But the authorities
have already been alerted
and everyone is pointing our way.

An English Play

For five minutes
I make my mother read
The Tempest aloud.
A lullaby, I say,
if you do it right. I pin
her finger down and the ship
rocks to its side, prostrate,
chewed and spit out
in the Captain's voice, you,
the army of fleas and this, life,
this is life crawling overboard
and I dragging I blazon
I birth forth the first word.
My gift to her,
lucky, saucy tongue,
straight, pearly teeth
and elegant, slender throat.
We can lop mountains in two,
spring rivers from the ground
and make water thirst
for the path I flick, flicked
into shape like the hoary
dragons we are. *Louder*, I say,
and louder she sings because
I am so very powerful.

It Even Had Holes Where a Bird Had Been Holding It

Today, I searched for a dying rat
I saw last week on my way
from the doctor to the butcher,
but when I found it and saw
the ants, I could not touch it.

Their heads were fearsomely oversized
and they crested their summit as one
eusocial tide flooding a hill of grass
the colour of fur.

In this species, workers cannot be told
from soldiers, though the queen is
as invisible as ever, safe somewhere
within the chest cavity.

Fur shivered and the world
holding tight to the roots
of its blades was a beast–
the dying rat showing signs
of it being alive.

A few moments more
of wanting solitude.

An unitchy end.

An unirritating life
in which it had never been

...

airborne. Had never flown
or tasted blue sky.

After such heights, does it matter
how it made its way
into the cardboard box?

When who touched who
and electricity was conducted

a love shock

it's been called

which skin was the skin
harboring extra electrons
and how critical was the rain
soaked fur to the harm
our private moment contrived?

I did not even know that yesterday
meteors were falling.

To Reach in Only for the World to Shift

There is a stuffed bear stuffed in my bra waiting
with no sudden movements until parts of me loosen
and she smells more like me. *Nothing of substance*,
she whispers to me, leaving my maternal body
behind with other, old furnishings. A tidy pile,
its readiness to burn smelling like spilled milk,
or milk coming too fast for a nose sewn in umber
thread because my bones have stopped prioritizing
bone density over plastic pellets that give way
like fish shoaling to the hand squeezing too tight.
It's no accident that our first reflex is a strong
and blind grip. When you are all intention,
there's little ground left for the cover of weeds.
It's been so long since thunder has woken me
from fearful dreams and homespun vestments
that I had forgotten the wider grief of wilder skies,
only remembered that weeds as toxic as daphne
require rubber gloves that will have to be thrown out.
I might want more permanent fixtures than nightlights
and darning a fourth, a fifth time, but by *accident*
I meant a moth larvae's hungry mouth, not the stain
spreading across my chest for the fourth, no, the fifth
time today. For thinner air I might give up the scent
clinging to me, my *eue de toilette—*
your mother is me, your mother is here, so drink.

A Long Time Coming

The lychees that make their way to her after many oceans, many lands, and a cultural revolution
are green, their plains of horns, softer than they should be. She knows just where to squeeze,
which pressure point along the shoulder girdle will make them shiver, just as she knows
she's starving when she buys for seven dollars a pound, tennish bags. The fruits warped inside.
Their vascularity, hard, and the rot they drip, a foggy matter. Disintegrations of wood, small
and dark, lie bitterly within each navel indent. She, a sac of sugar's destiny. She, stowaway,
living in a cul-de-sac for confused identities and devotees of Confucius who are, themselves,
anachronisms. Being born of a lychee tree means not surviving the advent of televised adverts
in colour, means not affording the entrance fee to markets enamored by ancient's enameled wares.
Safety from bruising needing more than righteousness and curiosity (more than an immigrant's
woes), the few she's readied for eating are not ready to eat. But before her moonly tears can
chance making a run for the waterways, back the way they came, the lychees have their sweet
way with her. From the whites of two eyes, a lily grows. It floats up, rising to the third story
where it moves like a ghost, scraping against windowsills and knocking over pots of irises.
Behind each pane, a street of uneasy sleepers dream confounded expressions closer and closer.
They fall for her leftovers. Empty rinds and storms of dust.

The Taste of Things

There were words my mother
never taught me

juniper
hamlet
stucco
junco

They filled us up
these unspoken words
neither of us knew

Eventually quiet
broke open

A tree meaning nothing
to us broke it

Kept its sex
in grey-blue berries

Offered us a drink
said, here

Here is some of the bitterness
without which we had lived

A Group of Sixty-Seven

after Jin-Me Yoon's *A Group of Sixty-Seven*

It was not my place to wonder at the gleam of sixty-seven
Asian busts whose backs are turned to me. Not my place
to wander the balustrade a downward dog, my lolling tongue
dragging across balusters, concrete, tasting of vitamins
or a teat of the-brush-off. When the gatekeeper asked,
How much would you like to pay? I said, *Five*, because
I'm in the process of mitigating my water bill, taking
my showers to my grandmother's condo for assisted living
where I taught the old mule her second pledge of allegiance,
the names of the fifty states she's allegedly a citizen of
and the four most recent presidents. In return, she taught me
how to pick a neighbor's tree clean of its nickle-sized plums,
lay fertilizer down in the cover of night, then contribute
such a jumble of identities that I loom over the block
like a bowheaded whale, my bowed-at-the-waist neighbors
spread like termites or a pile of tiny jars of jam stolen from
the Victorian hotel downtown. She is the one who made me
so grand and loving, so ready to cuss in a thick language
the sixty-seven Asian busts whose backs are turned to me.
Any gleam must be the film in my eye, not the plastic
sheathes keeping them dry. Sixty-seven women and men
post shipment. Post settlement in the art of a new country,
their eyes fixed to brown and green figureheads: tall trees
in a painted forest, before taller women and men clear-cut
a path for them to the gallery wall that every painting
to ever grace this province has hammered steel nails through,
reaching with rust the guts of plaster in what has been accused
a performance of ambition. Asian figures asked to dress

themselves before their upper thirds are transferred to
an instigator like moi, before their feet are saved to walk
home in the open road after a shoot pays them to get silly
on Emily Carr's aged, acrylic fumes, faint and unpleasant
were it not for the metal frame enclosing each bust with
its muse as if they were confessing. A race on repeat
racing to wear nice but not ridiculous shirts, ties, prints,
open jackets, obvious silk and one costume, pink and Korean,
all of it lying in a pile at the back of my closet of skins.
Which shirt would I have worn? Would I have been naughty
and licked the lead off the painting? It's an original, you know.
What if it tasted like nothing you could have predicted?
If it tasted like future crime?

Labours of Translation

Like a bivalve dug out by a metal spoon
that spent its first life scraping cartilage
from the precocious kneecaps of athletic
young women, and its second
in a graveyard, atoning, I am
part of a nation's ingestion plan.

I am breathing more naturally
than the clam waiting for death
not knowing death is coming.
Waiting for the universe, which
likes to work in mysterious ways,
to be too fatigued to gorge
on linguine ai fruitti di mare.

What comes out of my mouth
bidden and sculpted
by a wet, fleshy muscle
are the words I need
when they are needed.
In the next life, they will
be capable of flight
and not have to worry
about being dug up.

But first, their first life, spent
in another language and spoken
as a question. We all have to find
ways to pass the time till reincarnation,
so I write about my parents because
they say my parents are not so important.

Over the counter, the cashier says this
to me after my parents ask for something
to be grilled. He says this to me without
understanding my parents when they say,
The oil he uses for frying cannot be trusted.

When my parents need a new phone
and are owed one by T-Mobile
for a plan that comes with
100 messages, 1000 minutes
of calling and a new phone,
they say this to me.

When my parents are not happy
with the price they are quoted,
they say this to me and sometimes
I listen.

Sometimes I say to my parents,
This is good enough.
Here, is a good deal.

But then my parents notice our WiFi
is not as fast as the numbers the slip of paper
they slipped under our door has printed
in gargantuan Helvetica, so I hear it again,
Your parents are not worth writing about.

They say this to me when they
do not know that I can hear them.
They do not say this when they
let me play with their daughter
and feed me chicken nuggets.

They give me a new phone, unlimited
minutes for my inconvenience,
fibre optic speed and a set of crystal
chromosomes. They grill me a filet
of tilapia, a side of the day's vegetables,
then everything else.

Nothing Grows in This Heat

Warmed blood quickens everything
from metabolism to lovemaking
while you and I perform a pile of honeybees
schlepped off to the monoculture

debating our perishing on the field
of nutrients that is blueberry pollen,
that is not enough once the last hedgerow
and its wildflowers have been cut.

With *Nosema ceranae* sieving
our minds like we have
more to lose than we do,
we fly past our duty

to never return when
I'd rather us look
like a flight of geese
arriving from out of town,

and if not that then a video
of starlings in murmuration,
hypnotic and mostly free,
after you did that sweet thing

yesterday with the old lady
and her cane,
the double-decker bus,
the frigid lake,

the plugged seat belt,
the sharp teeth,
and the mouth-to-mouth
lubrication.

You and another lady
while I was searching the aisles
of Publix for peanut butter
and some awful gourd

of your childhood.
When its stringy, blah flesh
bubbled up our neighbor's sink,
I knocked and knocked

but the old man wouldn't
open up and let me
push a coiled snake
down his drain.

This, standing outside
my neighbor's door
holding a butternut casserole
is my alibi.

I'm being as serious
as refrigerator light.
I was there.
I saw you go slack

on the woodpile,
your head cocked,
your gullet bulging
after one too many

beetle larvae.
Anything could
have gotten you.
A cat, a hawk.

The Congee Test

My mother's congee may look strange to you
at first, but is really just seven portions bone
broth boiled with one cupful of rice for the white
marrow and white starch she calls silk and we call
velvet. It's not as strange as the sea and its giant
squids and anglerfish; its colouring, though pale,
has never reminded you of the sea's wife, the moon,
even with her black hair pulled back, *oh what*
a nape, and bound in a hairnet like a good professional.
If not the tide schedule in laminate or our undigestible
beak, left behind in a sperm whale, call it a pond
if you can hold your favourite pond in both hands
to serve my blondish auburn boyfriends their dinner,
where cast aboard our leafed-out table you'll find
our slipperiest chopsticks, our inmost bowls and oval
plastic plates, their red temple drawings hidden
under piles of delicacies we never ate: horses, shark fins,
jellyfish and the translucent tendons of a pitbull mutt
gone limp in black vinegar.

If my appetite surprised you after nights
of reassurance, *I'll moan when you moan,*
if I stroked your hand, *Thank you for this bag*
of Werther's Original, then swallowed you
and your smile, all of us smiling, remember it was
an accident. Me meeting you and you finding me
very beautiful. When you balked, then bucked,
I looked away, gave you your privacy, a paper towel
halved, a stroke underneath the table, then a test
in the textures of golden treasure.

Holding something small and grey for me
by the tips of her chopsticks, my mother said,
This one would not eat the shark though it flailed
on the sea's floor for three days to be served
on my table. You were already home scoring
loaves of bread, *I told you, we don't eat sourdough*,
and she was at the sink sifting leftovers in moonlight,
trying to catch us by the slivers of shark you had buried
beneath a blurred and pockmarked congee face.
So I turned away and left my mother in her kitchen.
My mother who would never understand how things
in this country were very gruesome.

But now, what if I told you I have just lied?
That the whole time it was me
and I've grown tired of choosing
between duck tongue and the tongues
of blonde boys. Tired of replacing more
and more of a recipe's all-purpose white
with whole wheat until it collapses.
Or overproofs. These days,
I sit in front of my TV
and dream about butterscotch.
Butterscotch coating my throat,
butterscotch dripping down
the tail of my back,
butterscotch in my pants.

Afterbirth

my mother was invented
from a bend
in the lintel

before plate armor
and Mao's red Mars
made it to their roundings

before even protective spells existed
and embroidered belts were stroked
for their softness

before extenuated generational learning
rubbed the fat part of her palms
into gunwales

old dirt of
a new home

can protuberance till
the wind catches
make ghosts

because of her
many wonderful
and terrible things know
their orbiting capacity

I defer
a narwhal can swim
in a beluga family

didn't we all
our daily lives skulk
from one corner
to another

I defer
a moo is happening
by leaping
over short
stone walls

walls that are low because
they are famine-built

a government circuit
of soup and stone
soup and stone

I defer
her calf is two pastures
from the slaughterhouse

I defer
her calf has her
leaping over stone
walls because
scents have a way
of finding their way
back to you

the long tusk
belligerently interruptive
is eerily familiar

or familial

trailing behind toddlers
who tower from seats
made out of bowed shoulders
and gleaming views
of their daddies' bald crowns

I defer
they are fine

never fined
talked back to

given lip
at the swing set

metal and so
stereotypical

migration so orbicularly
quiet

so
after the fact
astounding

Maternity Leave

It's worth pointing out
roadkill.
Worth slowing down,
pulling onto the shoulder,
stepping onto gravel
and hearing the crunch
of free to arrive and free
to take leave.

Looking for Jade Rabbit

I reach inside your skull
and stroke a special spot
push my finger in so the farthest
curve of my nail
sinks just slightly
until you forget God
just
I will
hold
God
for a little while

yes this is violent

what you are smelling is bone opened up to its sapwood

the myrrh is dribbling out nicely

do you want me
to stop
I can tell you things: the moon inside
your head
looks like a moon
the priest is calling the children up
wait
tell me what is he holding
what did I miss

Ziploc bags of Goldfish
have you ever

crawled beneath pews
sipped the Gulf
what should I do with your God
tell me
God
is the breeze bothering you
I can turn the AC off we like to sweat
is my nail bothering you
that is intimacy I'll let go
in a little
while

Husbandry

If you don't know what to do for the wasp
that has fallen to the dregs of your
morning coffee, call me,
and I will lend you my husband.

He will come right over, teach
you about a mouth of warm air
and what one from you to her
can do. Easy, you think to yourself.

But then he'll ask you
to get close to her only defense
before opening your mouth wide,
which is more difficult.
But for the sake of dry wings,
you do as he says.

He won't be able to help himself
from explaining how your sacrifice
was not for her exterior
but for her fragile interior,
chilled by even the briefest
of drownings.

Then, in the quiet, as you
watch the thing you killed
recover on the arm of your chair,
I honestly do not know
what he will say.

Keep him even so.

For as long as you like.

Or as long as he is good to you.
At least, until she is warmed
and sleepy in your hand,
ready to eat whatever
you can bear abandoning.

Hometown

Chongqing undresses us
for an affair that requires more
brilliant and higher voices than
what we brought with us,
a warble to slink into second
bedrooms and viciously
expensive sorghum liquor.

The man watching me is small
and wearing a pair of glasses
we brought with us, along
with two boxes of Epsom salts,
socks shedding silver strands
of mohair, and warming gloves
that came with their own energy cells.

He is taking care of me
in the corner of my mother's eye
where chummed up tea leaves
distract us; their flat, adhering faces
flushed from their lusty
grips by a porcelain lid
whose flicks

clink the side of her
vessel's lip. He still
loves my girlish mom
so he shepherds her daughter's
rhythm of sips and cooks
for us from his garden:
dark green leaves, easily bruised,

bouquets of watercress,
ginger I didn't need
to peel. An overwinter
propagation kinder
than the one they,
he and my mother
had honed to holes

in the countryside,
where each tuber eye
was cut out and buried.
How to plant each one
far enough apart
when you're starving
with only the wet knife to lick–

this, the magic trick.
Like a boy who
never learned to drive,
buying a new car to pick
my mother up from
the airport in.
Like my mother

who hated to drive,
driving from the airport
to her hometown,
stopping
at each light,
and moving on
when they turned.

Why I'm Named After a Stranger

You're my personal pizza, she says,
in the tale of coming here
with a capital H, oozing
from Texas into New York,

then Cali,
then wherever North Dakota is,
like a pocket bursting
from five fives. Not her pocket

but the baby-oiled stranger
who bought my mother
her first personal pizza.
The whole world for a five.

Her face is still lit by garlic crust
when the real child turns two
and starts peeling food away
layer-by-layer:

the pepperonis first,
the onions and peppers,
even the melted cheese,
before stopping

at its saucy, red dimples,
content with devouring
their wettish,
whitish foundation.

One of the Catadromous

Most learning will be from *how little.*
Like how little a little girl is or how
little girls come into their elver selves.
Everything to do with
how little we know.

As a little little girl my education,
my task of toil, was to sketch for
the abyss of ignorance, cliffsides
and impassable boulder fields.

To understand the human
condition, I was to shock
the moray eels to life and follow
the secrets they carried,
through three transformations
of body to frigid seas.

I was to paint the American chestnut tree
in mis-en-scene and in the cover
of its resurrected shade, wait
for insight priced at delicate lace,
embroidered shirt collars
and better cooking.

Critters, mollusks, crustaceans
invaded my Eden while I waited,
the mud teeming with life.
Tired of stoichiometry and pin pricks
I welcomed these creatures, busy

and uninterested in my solo speech:
the once crushing cyclops trying
for more meaningfulness, more prehistory
with any nearby mover, twitcher or trifling eater.

Marooned on this heavenly island
of paradigmatic shipwrecks
and sodden, bashed hulls,
waiting for the pots and waterskins
to drift their way to my shores,
I croon like a long-haired
inquisitive woman
for the grey squirrel I am watching
collect moss off a balsam fir.
Both now growing without my leave.

For the pennyfisted god surveying my island
with binocular vision, I write a paean
to make the little squirrel almsgiver:
its collecting, dole collecting,
then wait impatiently to be discovered
for my body parts and the shrub drinks
I know how to make well after living
in overgrown places.

The first place I am taken to
when I am rescued off my island
is the men's smoking lounge.
There there are knees for spreading
damp ringlets across to dry—
their hour, the midnight hour
of dark chambers lit by firelight
to better de-dust old growth desks.

The hour of my view, the carpet's
view. The taste in my mouth,
cleaning vinegar.

That hurt,
I say on the playground
and again,
and again.

Because there is an island I know
exists, with everything a complicated
life cycle requires: dew, a gulf coast,
a wild river, trenches of mud, the open sea,
sunlit gardens of seaweed.

Anagrams of a Documentarist

I've taken a hundred shots of my husband, elaborately, in costume,
the cactus pear his prop in this unpretentious, reluctant duettino
between aspiring photographer and peaceful domestic:
purple bedsheet-draped Himeros, one nipple looking just a little contused
for its doeishness, and his misery, of unripe fruit and strobe lit cocoons, seduction
jarring free *lover* from dry, desiccated *artiste* body. Sapped lids and a timeout,
I am filled with trouble for taking him to a farsa and asking him to dance,
as interested as the world of contemporary art is with humans and their stunted
humannish movements. Awkward, adorable creatures. *Your moaniest*
please my promise to make making love less exclusive. So please unsmite
Masahisa Fukase, who drank down a fatal flight of stairs after photographing his domine
for fifteen years. Even wives, it's true, divorce. Even black birds in the light of doctrine
can make an immodest book. It's late as I take care of the felled and gutted pears, unmount
them from the posing stool and lay them, for the pleasures of the sparrows and tufted titmouse,
in the field I have driven to as my husband sleeps. Having closed his eyes and gone mute
after we argued and couldn't stop, about time's destruction in a wine glass and the dustmen
who littered golden candy wrappers to make our living room shine, an inmost

change that struck us, sadly, different. But in this morning's shoot I found there are tines of light that make his tense face look beautiful. Rectangular, sharp-edged, they are the count of plastic blinds that fold like a fan, the cloudless day and an eye reclining on an arm's soft web, ready to take me, coolly, for its student.

At Least He Didn't Die in a Car Accident

Or by way of humping a dead shark,
all of us jealous of the brazen thief
who had given up retinol and sunscreen
to conquer baby soft smoothness between
his naked knees. From his thrusting
sunburned back—a viral video on loop—
we learned that our skin was not as soft
as marine life, our livers were not buoyant
and sitting inside us were stones that would,
one day, drown us.

I can tell from your disinterest in lovemaking
that you are not with me, here, but in grief,
elsewhere, your eyes drifting
from the screen, tracking a robin.
You have been so long along grief
that you've written a book about insects
who deserve their apiary crises, their lost way,
their *Nosema ceranae*, their pauses
on every front lot garden, their ramble down
every side interest – naming hurricanes,
collecting visas, fishing, legally –
when the best thing to do while waiting
for an inquest is to go on a walk, with me.

We'll stop by the bait store and take the turn
that is more private, onto the longer road,
until we reach the banks of Cayuga River
where, fingers deep in fathead minnows,

....

you'll get distracted like suburban wildlife
turned nippish while I, already in the water,
call out for you to hurry.

On land, there'll be a loud kerfuffle.

A unicorn will butt your elbow,
trying to stick its horn in your minnows.

You'll get annoyed.
You'll swat its snowy cheek
and it will step back to look at you,
as if to ask if you're sure.

You'll say, without thinking,
Scat, be gone.

Antinomian in the Dark

1

everything can be crystallized to the good cheating my mother escorts around the room,
her silver tongue wagging, working a silver-plated brass platter of hors d'oeuvres, hosting
like it's in her blood or someone made her out of glass, a greenhouse in Nevada: generous
with its space and light and opportunistic like a homeless being, like pea shoots, like a witness
to manmade famine.

2

I once read a poem by a child of immigrants about the Amazing Duo of Immigrants the child
of immigrants was born to and could not but whisper loving whispers to myself: *mine were better,*
so better. they were taller and quicker. they were smarter and could convince you of anything.
like my father might not even be my real father. somewhere my father could be anywhere.
in some times and places I might be the reason she needed to marry him, the reason
she needed insurance: homeowners, autobody, medical.

3

a girl sees all the families, all the big families of this country. she is invited to their
Thanksgivings and Christmases, and she says yes, usually, and sits at long tables

eating more than anyone else. she finds the laughter too quick to follow. things that
are not funny are funny and things that are funny are lost in the clamor that is not her
because she is an orphan and orphans are always quiet, even when they have mothers
who text every morning, "*how last night sleep, my darling*?" so when her friend
looks over to check on her drowsy awe, before looking away to do something ridiculous,
like bite into the shoulder before her, ducking when he roars, they think she's under
the table because she's afraid. she who can eat all the plums off a plum tree in the nicer
part of town. she who would murder every polar bear so that she can start forgetting them.
she who knows to store her mother's eyes in a box of mangosteens, the chilled purple orbs
so cold they weep.

With Much Preparation, Her Father Still Dies Not Wanting to Die

With much preparation, her father still dies
not wanting to die.

Having eaten thousands of tiny crabs
who thought they were each
the colour of grey sand
until someone saw the blues
in grey like the loose threads
of a flag flying for mercy.

Having studied a species going extinct
bend gossamer as it went.

Having known nothing about gardens
when he sold out his neighbor.

Having flown a jet that could make
jam from the remains of other jets:
jars and jars left stalling on a high shelf,
a pretty row labeled strawberry.

Having committed terrible
deeds that cannot bear listing.

Having moved to an unfamiliar country
for his last demotion, doled out by pale
hands completing their duties in the manner
of children who never know as they take

...

that they are taking anything, somehow
worse than the heyday days
of the red revolution.

Having had to be brutish to catch
what splashed in the creek.

All of this before a violinist played Bach for tips
across the street from a suburban cemetery.

That weekend, there were even plastic eggs
in the lilies, waiting to come alive
in the warmth aloneness sheds
like penny candy, to send him off
with foreign customs and wild rabbits,
to scrub his endocrine clean
and block his liver while something
near the hospital ceiling catches
his eye, something certainly there
but tucked out of sight,
his crying face no longer nothing
to scare children with.

To be clear one final time,
not a note of Bach played that day
was played for him.

You Spend So Long Working It to Tenderness

In April of this year, the camelias bloomed
a month too early and spent

the better part of their lives
under their own bushes, sweetening

the neighborhood with their slow procession
through the transitive stages of rot.

This has nothing to do
with Joan Didion except

that March I was reading her
book of grief and trying, so hard,

to catch myself, arrest myself even,
in a particular column of thought,

a habit that seemed to be forming.
Daring to think this ink, bone dry,

unbudging and made special,
this is The Expensive Grief Mixture.

Full of prestige and sheltered
in a cauldron until it was needed

by the most famous writer
to grieve that year,

then pressed to many pages
so I could have one for every

day of the week,
a placemat

for every meal.
So I could read her Sundays,

and Mondays too,
with bland roast

and cauliflower florets
blended, then whipped

for the bad heart.
In this edition

of blue-black iteration,
most of the letters

for forming words
were scratched

into her dead husband's
monitor screen

with a metal,
pointed nib.

Then into the dinner plate
with a painted fingernail.

Words uniquely pleasurable
like Alcestis and dust jacket.

The wonderous writing duo
before he was dead.

While I am married to a scientist
studying compound eyes

and damsel flies.
Had years to make him

my partner in crime.
To elevate him

from writing punching bag
to writing buddy.

When it's his turn to fall
to the dining room floor

and drift away,
between course one

and course two,
I will work his last

words around in my mouth
like one is supposed to do

in a desert, lost,
with a pebble.

I'm allowed to have
this daydream

because this May
came one May too early.

Before my humble ant-body
was tragedy,

my sponge cleaning
my dead,

my mandibles always picking up
and dropping soap,

before my exoskeleton
blew away in the wind

like run-off,
like surplus catfish,

like not remembering what
we're supposed to remember.

It's getting late and
I still have not

caught myself thinking
better her than me.

Little difference,
little knows

I know what I have
been thinking.

Like when a dear friend calls
because someone

has just called
to tell her that death

is fraying his first thread
in the bedcover

she's spent her days
embroidering.

I'm sorry,
I say to her.

Then, when the call ends,
Thank you.

Grateful for her bite
I bite my lower lip.

So quick, one call is,
yet so long coming for me

that May I finally earned
my night of restful sleep

beneath brilliantly dyed
and neat cross-stitches.

Thanks to Robinson Crusoe

Virginia Woolf once said
the pot is our protagonist and if we are
to be filled, we are to be empty,
and the pot, to be filling.

Wooden handles to be
better manhandled, throw
out the holy and the profusely
stewed and we will be

whatever you want, fit ourselves
inside the pot and eat bread
dunked in milk. *Thank you*, we'll say,
bread in milk is good for us.

Our mindsets tend to
populate islands
with the things we make,
and for the rest,

even the shipwrecked,
islands generally
have raisins, tortoises
and plenty of guinea fowl.

Such a minor thing it is
to be a little broken
in English, a little spoiled
like broken milk.

What they are calling
the whites of your eyes
is their reflection
slowly sinking,

before quicksand,
a friendly branch,
or the reins of a loyal palomino
can be read.

The Night

In her shrouded tent,
little children
unravel so sweetly
she spoils us
with cover.
When the sheet lies flat,
we are flattened.
From soles flexing
to our ribcage,
over our bended knees
to hips that haven't
yet complained
of their facing,
day after day,
the external.
We notice for the first time
the great shame
of the negative,
otherwise known
as the hole in my side.
The shore is close
and I am riding
in the ice chest
of a dingy,
slipping away

across the lake,
my fins splayed
as shudders dim
my smaller sight.
A curved hook is
a line still and wet
with one opening,
I dig into another.
Probing, probing, probing
I give Excalibur back
and on the other side,
pushed through
a thickened hide,
the shortest breeze
rustles through me,
and the warmest rain
rustles through me,
and the softest bell
rustles through me.
I lie myself down,
as close to the ground,
until sacred loses
interest.

Engines of Ingenuity, from the University of Houston, Printed and Read on Sunday Mornings, for Practice

When my mother says something
    incoherent,
the atmosphere becomes
    uninhabitable,

showing off how cleaved home
    can be while I lunge
for her drooping
    robe sash, a sashay

toward closeted dignity while
    we are cached
by exposition,
    my mother's unshucking.

The air exuded from *feasant*
    muttering, pulling
silksoft tufts by the root,
    the heavens trying

to shake off
    the bad taste in its mouth,
the roof taking off
    like a swan

painted white,
        the tornado siren
joining the banquet
        because we live in Texas,

where the walls
        are wagging tongues
and the neighbors
        can choke you.

Where the roof used to be
        the stars are running.
The Sun, Saturn,
        Jupiter's moons too.

A lake of vastness growing
        in this moment
she stops all sound,
        my mother

struck by such
        open jaws
of freedom
        she doesn't flinch

when I press on
        the latch in her,
her calf the other side
        of my little finger

preparing me
    for the moment
she gathers herself
    to vault

and skin seizes
    beneath skin.
Does she jump
    because

she knows
    the Rooster God
is overdue
    by minutes

with his intention to set
    time right
while I as luck luck
    luck *luck*

ignore the wall on my left
    as it crows
open a space
    large enough

for me to escape
    when the wall
on my right
    falls away

to the coyote,
      one end
of a shackle
      around its throat,

the other dangling,
      waiting.
My mother doesn't see
      what I see.

My mother has her head
      flung back,
shoulders moving with deep
      chokes of laughter

as her black horse hair,
      coarse and thick,
strong but
      unlovely,

whips about her
      in a wild crown.
A child turned
      tax collector,

I kneel for her
      safe keeping
as the world
      empties,

as the starving coyote
    leaps,
as the rooster crows
    that time

needs to be set right,
    as the jumbled rumbling
notices me
    under a starless night

and says
    in my mother's voice,
Correct me
    as I speak.

After You Started Taking Sugar With Your Tea

every so often, while you are writing,
taking what's left of the morning
for your comeuppance, after your daughter
clung to you too long at drop-off,
you'll hear a deadening thud
against the window on your right,
the window facing the willow tree
the owner before you planted
after her divorce. you'll slip
on your husband's boots because
you know this will be a short break
and you'll go outside to look for a small body.
you're already looking forward
to holding it in your hands
because you remember thinking, last time,
this is the softest thing you'll ever touch.
a siren is going off in the distance, getting closer,
bringing you back to the gravity of the situation.
there's a cedar waxwing somewhere,
dead or dying, and before the cats
and the coyotes, the ants and the flies,
the maggots and the beetles,
all it has is you.

Of the Sent-Down Youth

He had been luckier
than the rest of them.
Out of their class of six,
the only one sent to a field
of yams, the farmer
paid well for his keep
so that his stomach
would never hurt.
But it's a hard thing
for a sixteen-year-old boy
to eat last, only after
the farmer's family was done,
every meal for three years.
So the five of them agreed,
watching the lucky one
forty years later eat only
the heads of the crayfish
they were boiling in good,
thick garlic, that this was worse.
His father's clout a worse thing
than the thin, mountain soil
they had warmed with their bodies
laid down in spring.

My Uncle Robbed in America

my uncle rents a store, sells caramel chews and beer for ten years,
is Chinese King of the 25¢ sticky experience and Bud Light Limes,
speaks piss-poor English, twenty years, receives his first notice,
slid under the door, handwritten, needs translation.
my uncle owns packages of plastic packaging, is Convenience
Man or Convenience Uncle: watermelon delivered
to my house every Monday, the crispest day
of the week, or my uncle owns horseshit,
didn't have a boiled egg to eat, cried like a timer
whenever chopsticks hit the empty bowl.
my uncle talks brokenly, fifty years, serves
his American daughters breakfast, ten years:
eggs boiled in soy sauce, two a day, until a hunter
pays my uncle's landowner ten grand
so that my uncle's landowner will slide a note
under the door, handwritten, needs translation,
or translated, my uncle needs to sell five glass-front fridges
in a hurry, and in a hurry, a hunter is willing to buy
dozens for dimes to move into my uncle's store
before the month is through, though my uncle's daughters
rally their lawyer friends and my uncle,
having made it to the shores of prosperity,
wants back to where he came from,
or from eggs planted in thinnish soil spring
what the prologue called caramel chew
and hailed *small thinged King.*

He Soldered Track to Wheel

if there were ten ways to say kid in your language
kee-ad looking hooligan
kid with a bonbon
kid stealing chocolate
stealer of oranges in chocolate wrappings and other
diminutives

this for *chłopak*,
who swallowed the bull of an era
while it foundered in a boxcar
going mad, its spit
wetting you both:
look him in the eyes

guard his temples with good
wishes so his racking moans
can drive the wedge,
as if the plains of rye
were his to fret over,
so galling and obstinate

your memory of him
holding silverware in one fist
and in the other, chanterelles,
thin and slippery,
how hard it was
to digest silver down

...

into shit, the curse-word
already in the kid's name,
the kid who makes a mess
of things when things
are already a stinking mess
because the Soviets are stealing

trainfuls of toilet paper
and your beautiful,
rustful behemoth,
coming for you
on its wedlocked road
is bid to leave you behind,

toilet paperless,
potatoless,
what else could he do
but marry, your behemoth
to the empty furrows
of your land

A Son

My mother wants a son.
Any baby, she would say, I'll take any
baby you've got so long as it's a boy
baby, man baby, sweet-eyed
baby, don't get me wrong,
this bosom longing, this breastly
want, these soft hands are not
girl baby boinked, bunkered,
bumped off by babbling stream,
by washing basin, by old linen,
by the smell of garlic,
is not two daughters, sisters,
or the crow they called son, bad son
they'd say when the crow
tapped on glass, bad son
they'd say when the crow
dropped an egg that meant
too many gullets to feed,
our gullets going lax
the year that went bad,
that went dusty,
that showed us the character
of stuff, the actual density,
nutrients, atoms, constitution
of that which can be eaten
and that which cannot,
so the next year,
when we regretted
the last and went looking
for crows to chase,

we discovered the world
was crowless too
with things bigger than
a mother and her wants,
bigger than the coyote
with the sun at her throat
as she went for the calf,
bigger, even, than the sun
who wanted a different body
to dress in the light of day.

Done For

There is no reason for my sister to be dying in my dreams.
Yet comatose she lay last night and across her breastbone,
her hands at someone else's arranging formed a steeple.

A Pair of Sisters plying, in a painting, gowned adults
for more books and differential equations. She, the wicked
smart one, I think she was touched by a Catholic.

Draped in starched static and the hard lighting of hospice,
both torn from one gown and one booklet of instructions
for all the good reasons to die, she looks like Mary.

Her complexion, washed out. Or rather, carved into marble
with an infernal sore or two. I am saying infernal to you,
flickering brain, as you set fire to the room and try your escape

through the window. Even spread-eagle on the lawn like bad art
or the stone bench designed to bring comfort to nightmares
and the perkier of two bottoms, I still can't shut you up.

Not in this inner courtyard, where a universe is the louder
of two sisters going quiet before the other. I, the useless one,
left to a newborn world in which life moves forward

to the count of carcasses populating the road's shoulder,
repaved last summer. New religions meet the modern
era with new accouterments made out of polyester

but what regard do they keep for my sister? Here, now,
gravely talking around her prone form in white coats,
how do we delineate an animal stuffed with rice

from cotton batting? A tucked in sheet from numb toes?
Sisters from shared clothing? And if their love had been
a frenzy? A river of living salmon? If it be dammed?

My Folks in Autumn

everyone knows when it's pumpkin time   but me   and mine
imagine homely   innards tinged   blue-grey   and all the days
as if someone has forgotten   protective plastic is meant to be peeled
I did mean   to say someone   it wasn't me   you can still visit us
but be   forewarned   our lights are turned off   and you
golden leaves   you demise of splendiferous fog   you could trip
I don't know   much about you   but I welcome the cover
we've been left to   twilight   eucalyptus litter   bed of ball
cacti   there wasn't always   so much of me   I meant twilight
when I said plastic   so much laughing   like that painful joke
if you haven't seen a pomelo   you're in for a treat   or a scare
little connivance left   for an insult   for shared bread   husked

fruit   gluttonous sponge you called me   with a dabbing of bubbles
this   that time of year again   if you do   decide to come over
put your hat   on the HEPA filter   by the front door   brush the ash
from your coat   like it's dust   we will sweep   another time
only   please   don't track mud inside   only   please   cover
my mouth if I talk   in one   unbecoming language   I've been
put here   to translate   what am I   saying
oh   dear   I think   I spilled on you

Advertisements for Shaggy Brutes

Yesterday morning, her voice
was a sexy thing, a sly creative
grooming the base of her tail.
A cow, most days, other days
she was a herd of cattle huffing
for a stampede, her double coat
of woolly hair looking for bears
to chase, especially mama bears
to embitter her marble ribbing
with the charge of cortisol.
How can you not run sometimes?

She is not like me. I am the startler
in every grizzly foray. Scared shitless
when, startled, she sinks into my shoulder
and tosses me in a riverbed of smooth rocks
that have turned pink with salmon carcasses
laid open, their eggs squeezed from
their lengths for lazy tongues in a fashion
I can only liken, from within a small
and boring life, to spearmint toothpaste
beading on an electric brush head.
So here I am lying among tubes of toothpaste
while a grizzly with bad breath stands
over me, trying to decide if I am worth
scaring, in a mutilating sort of way, to death.

....

The circle of life is imminent,
but I see the stars just beginning
to appear, duskily, at the edge
of the camera's frame, a Nikon Z1,
and can only wonder, violently,
how all of these women are connected.
I thought of one and, years later,
thought of the other. Hardly enough
to write what I wrote about one woman
when I was another kind of woman.

> For a long time now I have loved whiteness.
> Whiter than winter melon, than Tammy
> my neighbor, white as some girl
> of my likeness and at least as white
> as if I could wear Tammy like a winter
> coat, her collar popped and her bottom
> swaying expensively, just above my knees.
> For now, I tell myself I shouldn't invite Tammy
> over for twice-cooked pork, only to salt
> her when she bows for the piece of meat
> I didn't meant to drop.

There was once a Highland Holstein,
spent to death from propping up
by her swollen hips EAT MORE
CHIKIN signs. Memories of forging
thunder having not yet leaked
from the cracks in her hooves,
in a braying voice she domesticates
herself, refusing to be left
in the open, in the lightning storms,
afraid to catch another cold.

Ripping into the nearest tree,
she rakes her hooves piecemeal
down sugar maple bark and hunching,
lumbers to another, whipping
her vocal cords to the edge of tensility
before she waits, ready to be run off
as if a threat.

The Dangers of Trying to Improve the World

The only time I ever committed deicide,
I killed the wrong god.
I know,
I know.

How could I so sin.
The only one we thought okay,
who walked with tigers
and pined for iteration,
the only one who wasn't a god.

Marvelous

after Edward Hopper's *Early Sunday Morning*

I'd like to rip something out
when I hear "collective American."
Not so there can be begonias
lining every ledge of this city
for out-of-towners.
In its reds, greens
and baby blues,
I try to recall
what the street
looked like, except
it is yours! It is yours!
Don't stop telling me—
I'm not keen for fighting,
at least not today.
The city is coloured vague
in my head with mixing,
blending oil paints,
contamination,
even love, but still
no one will let our shadows
squint the wrong way.
Let them be! So be it!
I can't hide so away
I will slither, the hissing
of the gas lamp lighting
our carriage ride home.
Who said the heart can sing?

I Eat Because I Can

I have spent my afternoon
declining calls from
the many boyfriends
I have made black silk

chickens for because, inevitably,
they keep calling for more,
their appetites for the next
generation not shriveling

like the purple-black skin
they so badly want.
Unusually univoltine,
my chickens refuse

the expectations
of my boarders
and hanger-on-ers,
not dying

quickly enough to protest
the changing seasons.
When winter comes
they stick to their coop,

take their time finding
old feathers to pull
for the tease,
Lady Anthropocene,

who curdled them with warm
mammalian kisses
when they were still closed
off from the world,

until they gladly pecked holes
out of their skies
and uncaved the roofs
stretching above them, lovely,

one continuous line
from modern, white walls
to ceramic for braising
long toes in black beans and sugar.

What conditions of birth
are ones such as these?
Never to eat like the lady finches
on the birdfeeder,

where small heads disappear
at an even clip
to a place where no one
can know with certainty

how much millet
is really being eaten.
The taste of privacy,
reckless,

and their leveraged bodies?
I see them shiver
as they lever in
and out of hunger.

ACKNOWLEDGEMENTS

Thank you to the generous editors of the following journals, in which poems, sometimes in earlier versions, first appeared:

Cathexis Northwest Press: "We Who Devour Pretty Things"
Cimarron Review: "It Even Had Holes Where a Bird Had Been Holding It"
Copper Nickel: "The Congee Test"
The Greensboro Review: "Let It Simply Be So"
The Ilanot Review: "My Folks in Autumn"
The Iowa Review: "Labors of Translation"
Iron Horse Literary Review: "A Long Time Coming"
The Lily Poetry Review: "He Soldered Track to Wheel"
NELLE: "An English Play"
PRISM International: "Looking for Jade Rabbit"
PRISM Online: "A Group of Sixty-Seven," 2nd Runner-Up of *PRISM International*'s Pacific Poetry Prize 2021
Quarterly West: "A Son of Wishes" and "The Taste of Things"
Salt Hill Journal: "My Uncle Robbed in America"
Zone 3: "Engines of Ingenuity, from the University of Houston, Printed and Read on Sunday Mornings, for Practice"

Thank you to my interminably brilliant reader and editor, Michael Prior. Thank you to the Anna LaBastille Memorial Writers Residency, the Sitka Center for Art and Ecology, the La Napoule Art Foundation and, most importantly, Cornell University, for providing me with the time, space and conversations writing this book required. Thank you Taylor Collier, Hillary DiLorenzo, Alice Fulton, Barbara Hamby, Christopher Hewitt, Ishion Hutchinson, Joanie Mackowski, Frances Revel, Sasha Smith, Lyrae Van Clief-Stefanon, and

Lindsey Warren, for all that you taught me and are still teaching me about the wild abyss that is language. Thank you to my family, for whom I am always writing: my gentle, noble father, Jacek Turski, my fierce, intelligent sister, Tingting Turski, and my mother, Jin Liu, whose luminous presence in this world has always been what makes it seem profound, astonishing and precious to me. Thank you Wendy and Michael for your generous love and care and all that you've taught me about trees, family and goodness. To my love, Leithen, without your mind, character and unending support, I would simply be lost. To my daughter, Dorothea, you've expanded my knowledge, heart, humor and happiness to lengths previously unimaginable to me, I love you dearly.

MICHAEL PRIOR, EDITOR
MICHAEL HARRIS, FOUNDING EDITOR

Robert Allen • James Arthur • John Asfour, trans.
John Barton • Doug Beardsley • Paul Bélanger
Linda Besner • Walid Bitar • Marie-Claire Blais
Yves Boisvert • Jenny Boychuk • Asa Boxer • Susan Briscoe
René Brisebois, trans. • Mark Callanan • Chad Campbell
Edward Carson • Arthur Clark • Yoyo Comay
Don Coles • Vincent Colistro • Jan Conn • Geoffrey Cook
Lissa Cowan, trans. • Judith Cowan, trans. • Mary Dalton
Ann Diamond • George Ellenbogen • Louise Fabiani
Joe Fiorito • Bill Furey • Michel Garneau • Susan Glickman
Gérald Godin • Lorna Goodison • Richard Greene
Jason Guriel • Michael Harris • Carla Hartsfield
Elisabeth Harvor • Bridget Huh • Charlotte Hussey
Dean Irvine, ed. • Jim Johnstone • D.G. Jones
Francis R. Jones, trans. • Virginia Konchan • Anita Lahey
Kateri Lanthier • R. P. LaRose • Ross Leckie
Erik Lindner • Michael Lista Laura Lush
Errol MacDonald • Brent MacLaine
Muhammad al-Maghut • Nyla Matuk • Robert McGee
Sadiqa de Meijer • Robert Melançon • Robert Moore
Pierre Morency • Pierre Nepveu • Eric Ormsby
Elise Partridge • Christopher Patton • James Pollock
Michael Prior • Medrie Purdham • John Reibetanz
Peter Richardson • Robin Richardson • Laura Ritland

Talya Rubin • Richard Sanger • Stephen Scobie
Peter Dale Scott • Deena Kara Shaffer
Carmine Starnino • Andrew Steinmetz • David Solway
Ricardo Sternberg • Shannon Stewart
Philip Stratford, trans. • Matthew Sweeney
Harry Thurston • Rhea Tregebov • Alice Turski
Peter Van Toorn • Patrick Warner • Derek Webster
Anne Wilkinson • Donald Winkler, trans.
Shoshanna Wingate • Christopher Wiseman
Catriona Wright • Terence Young